Unicorn Coloring Book

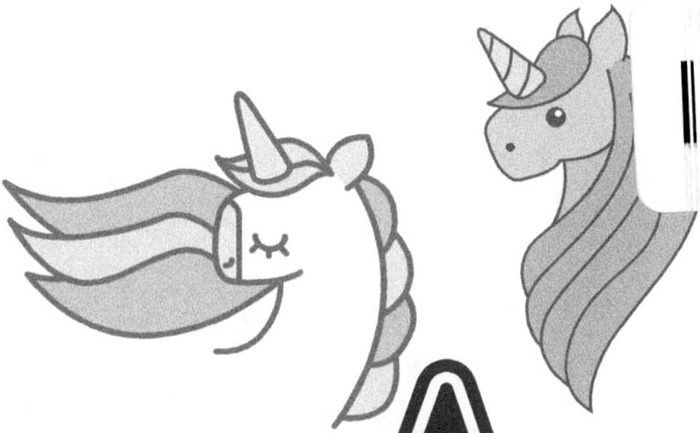

This book belongs to:

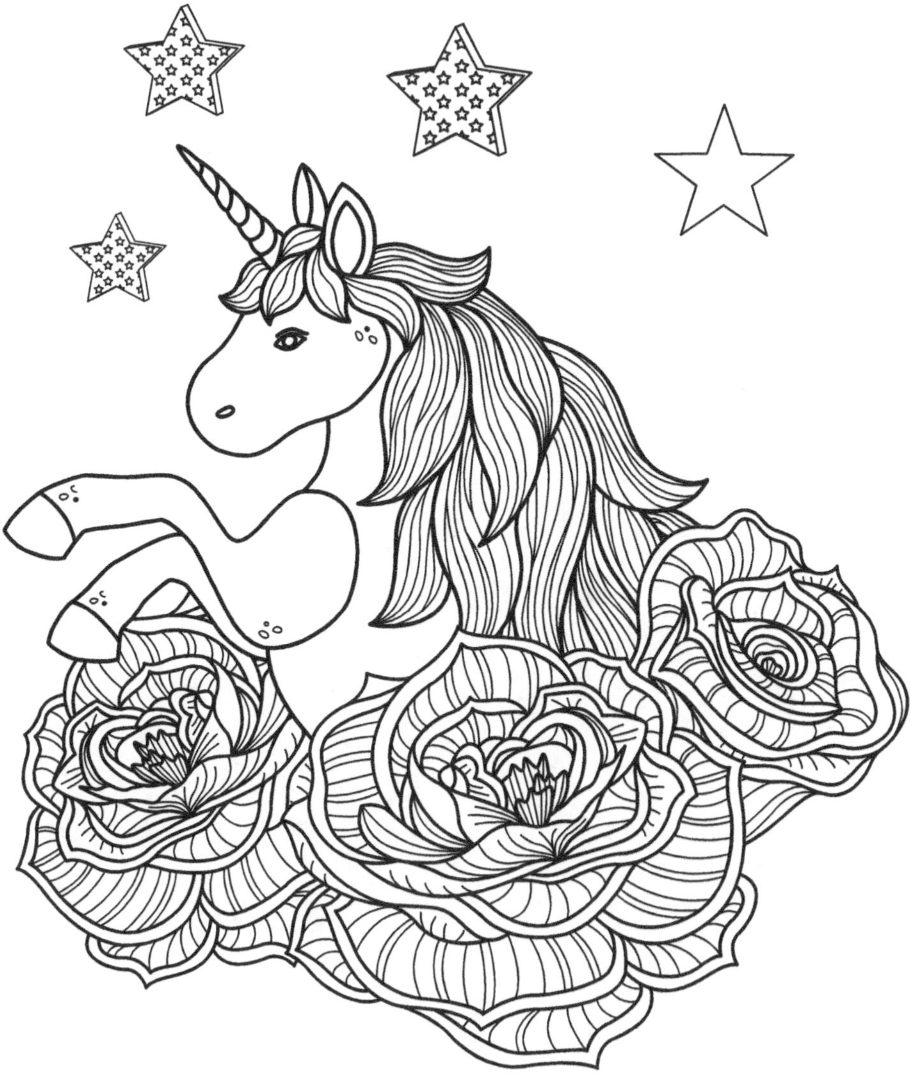

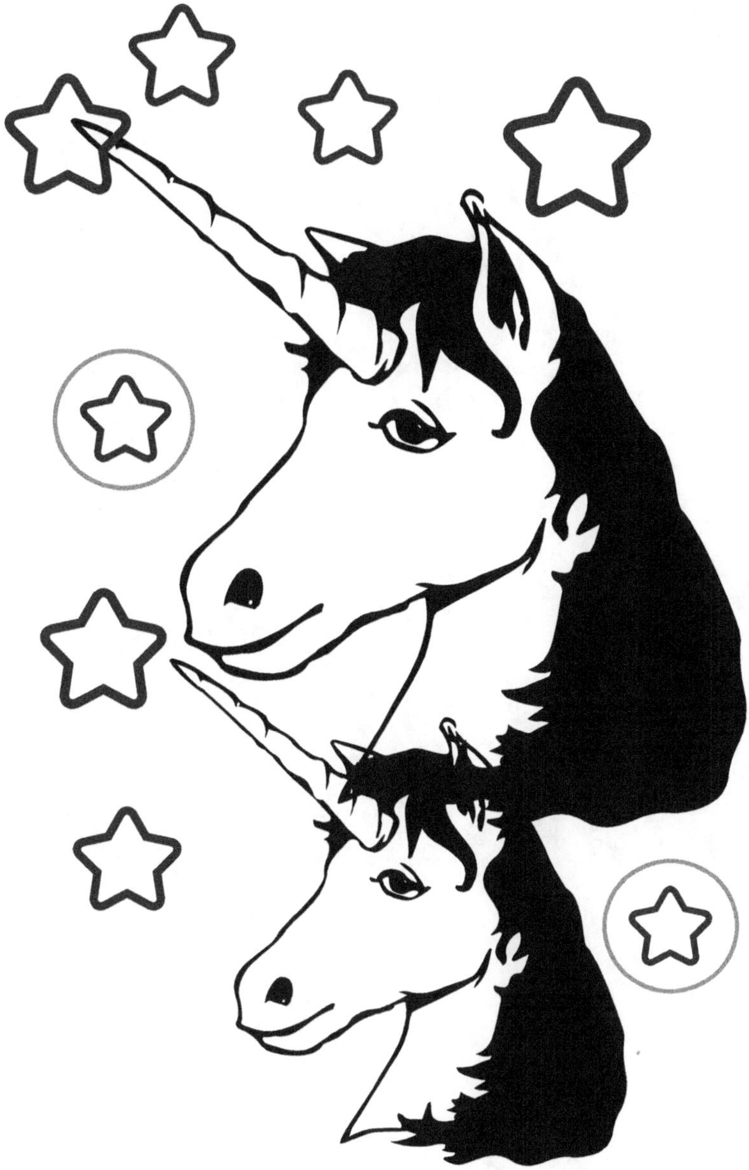

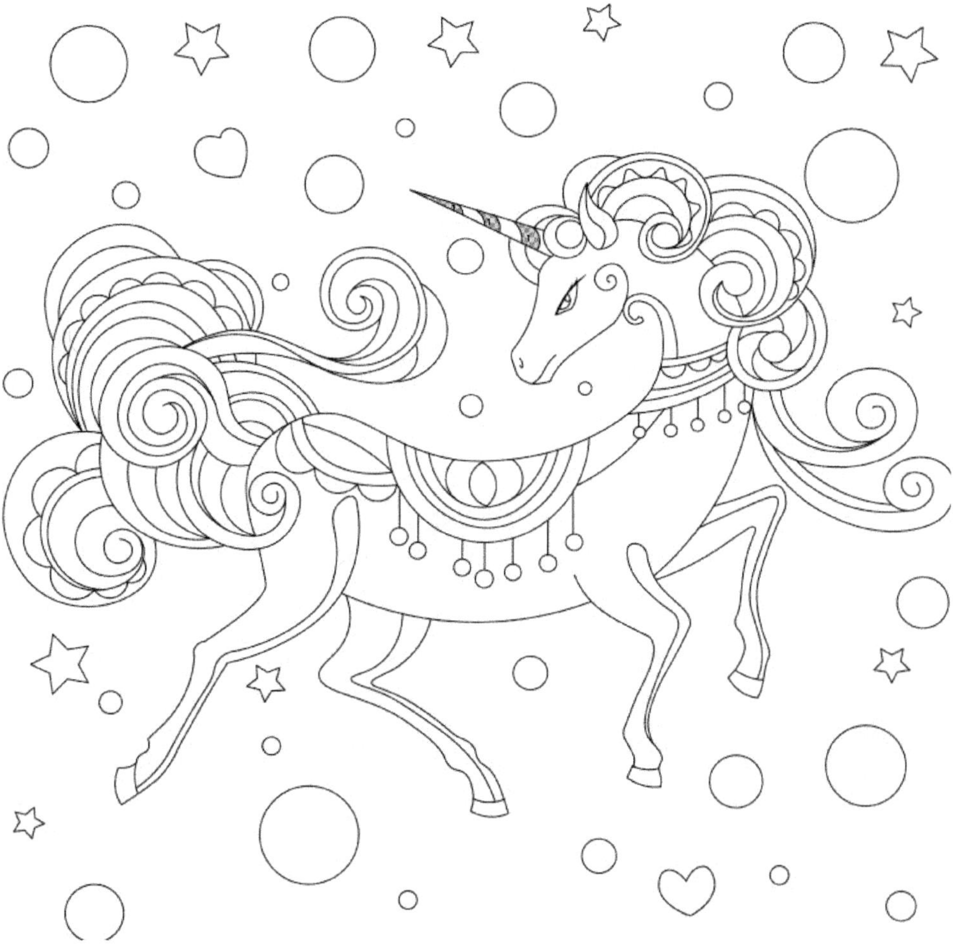

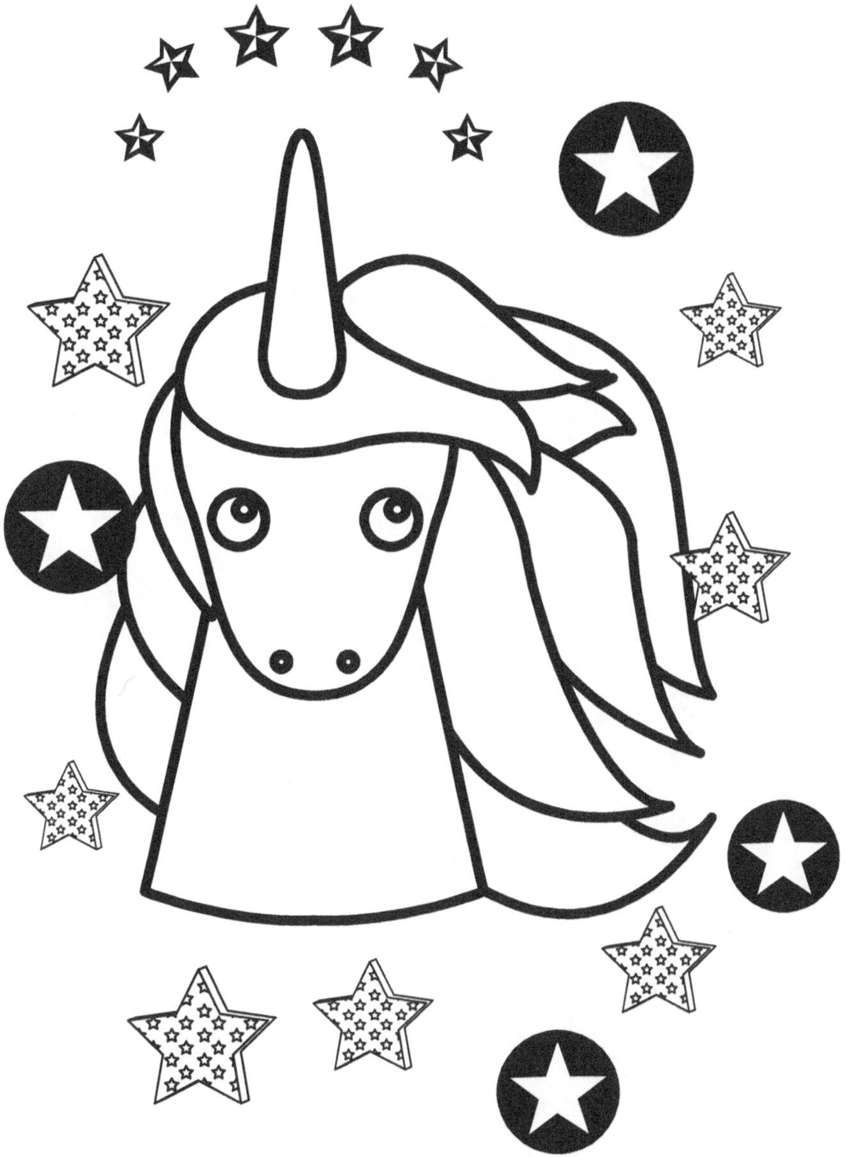

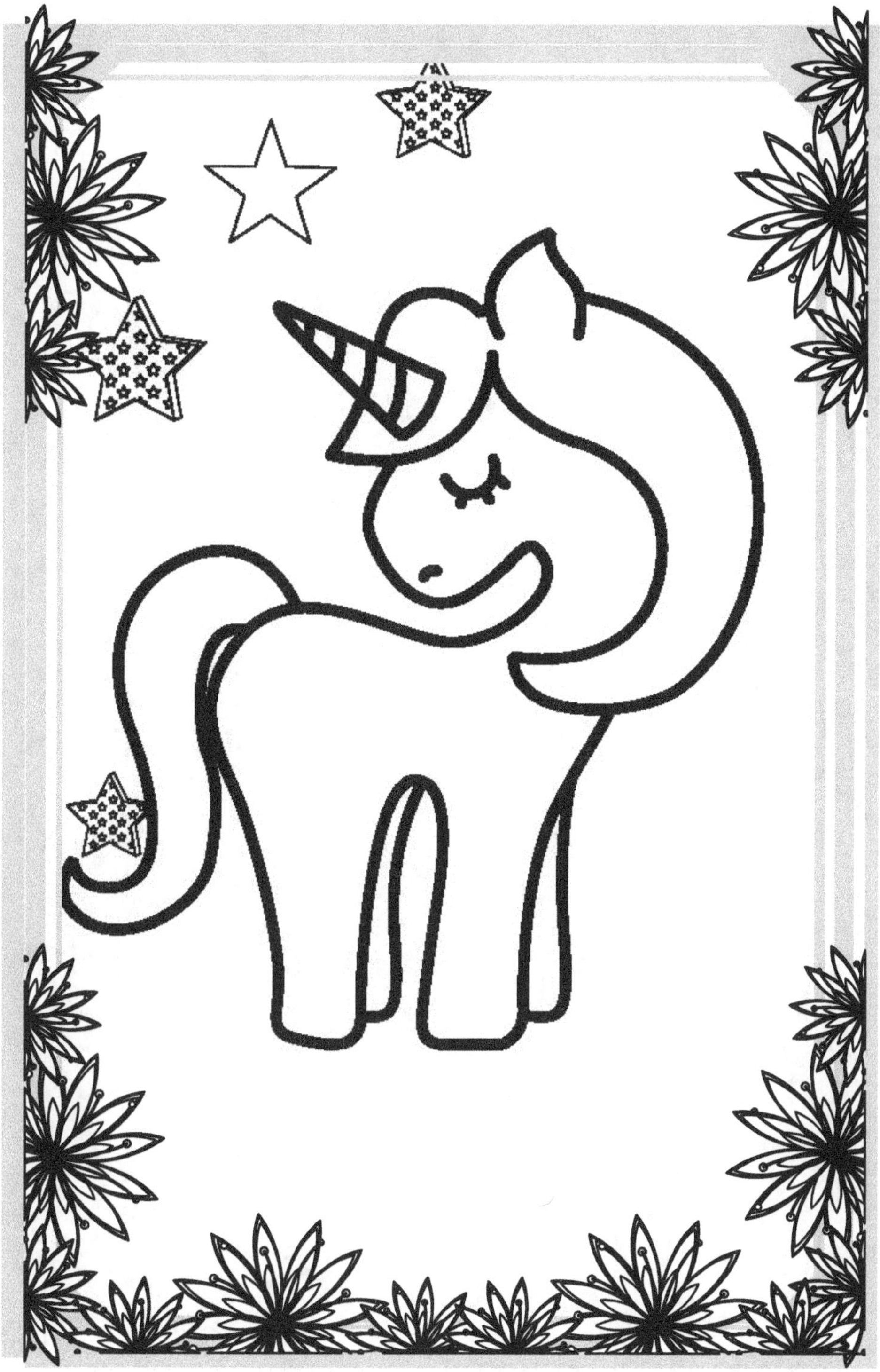

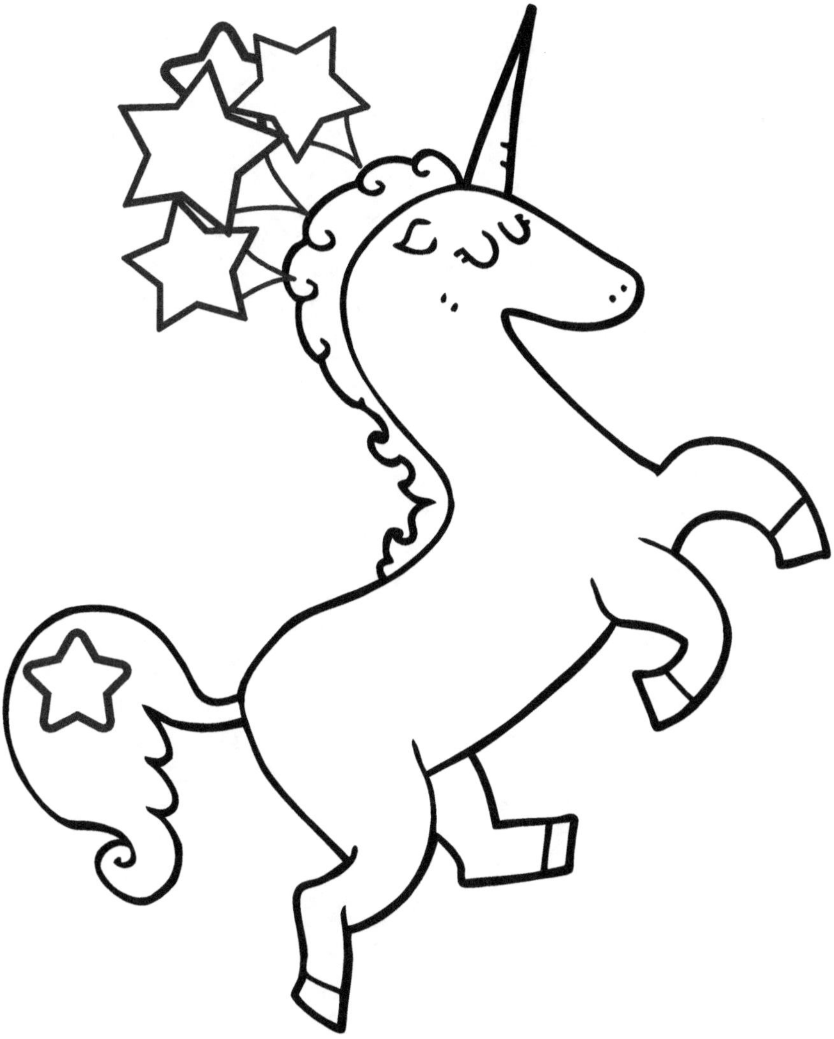

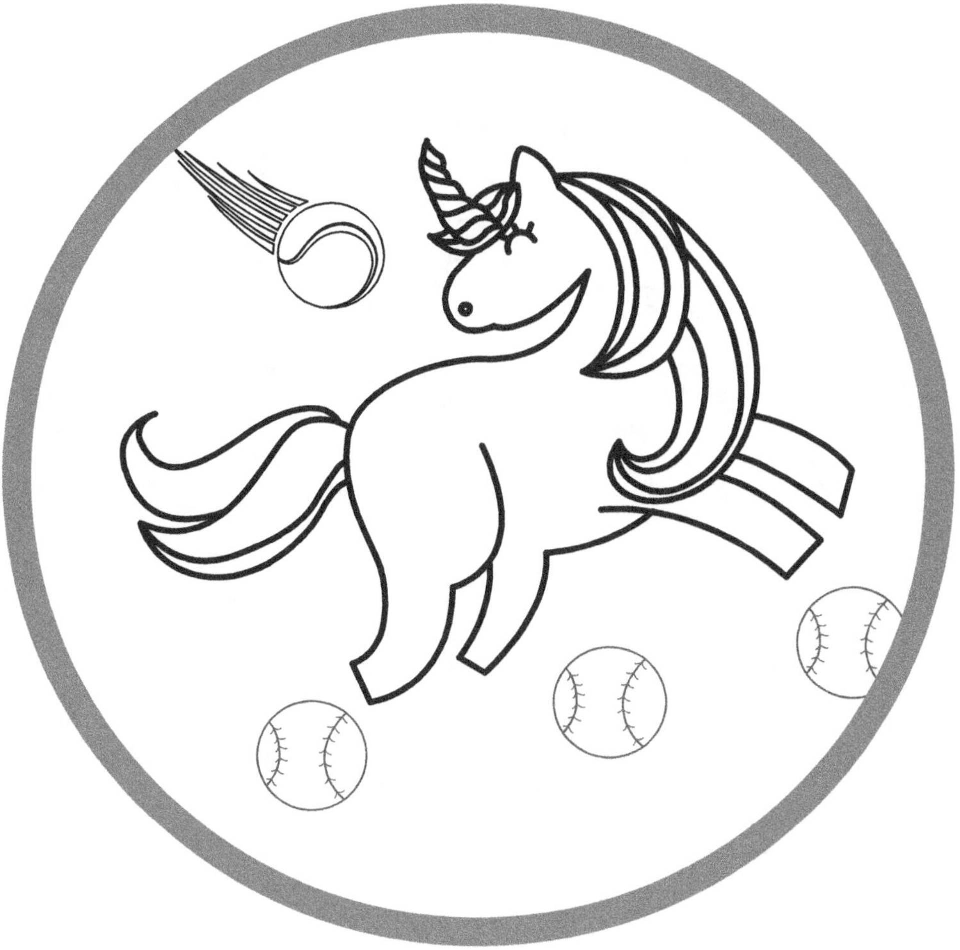

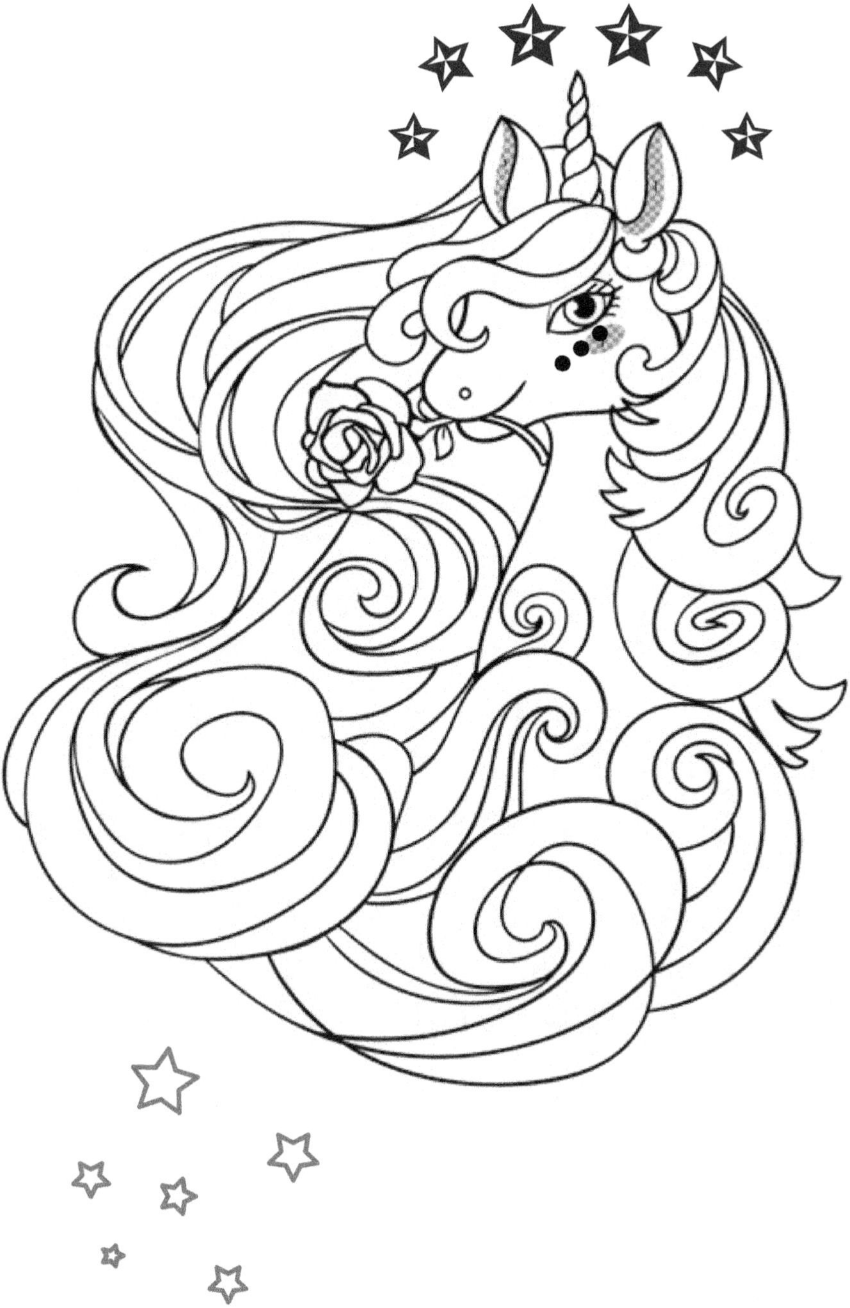

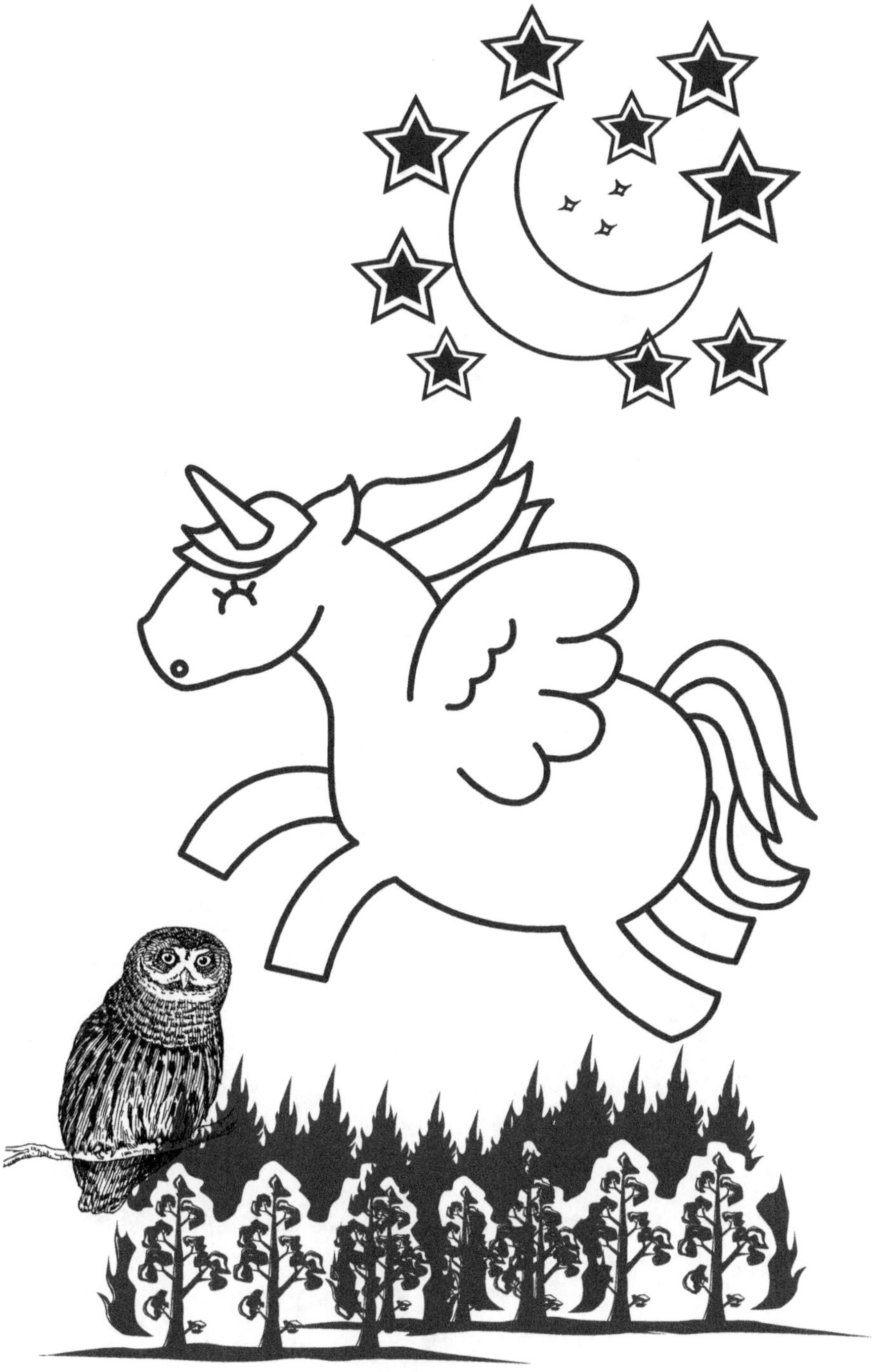

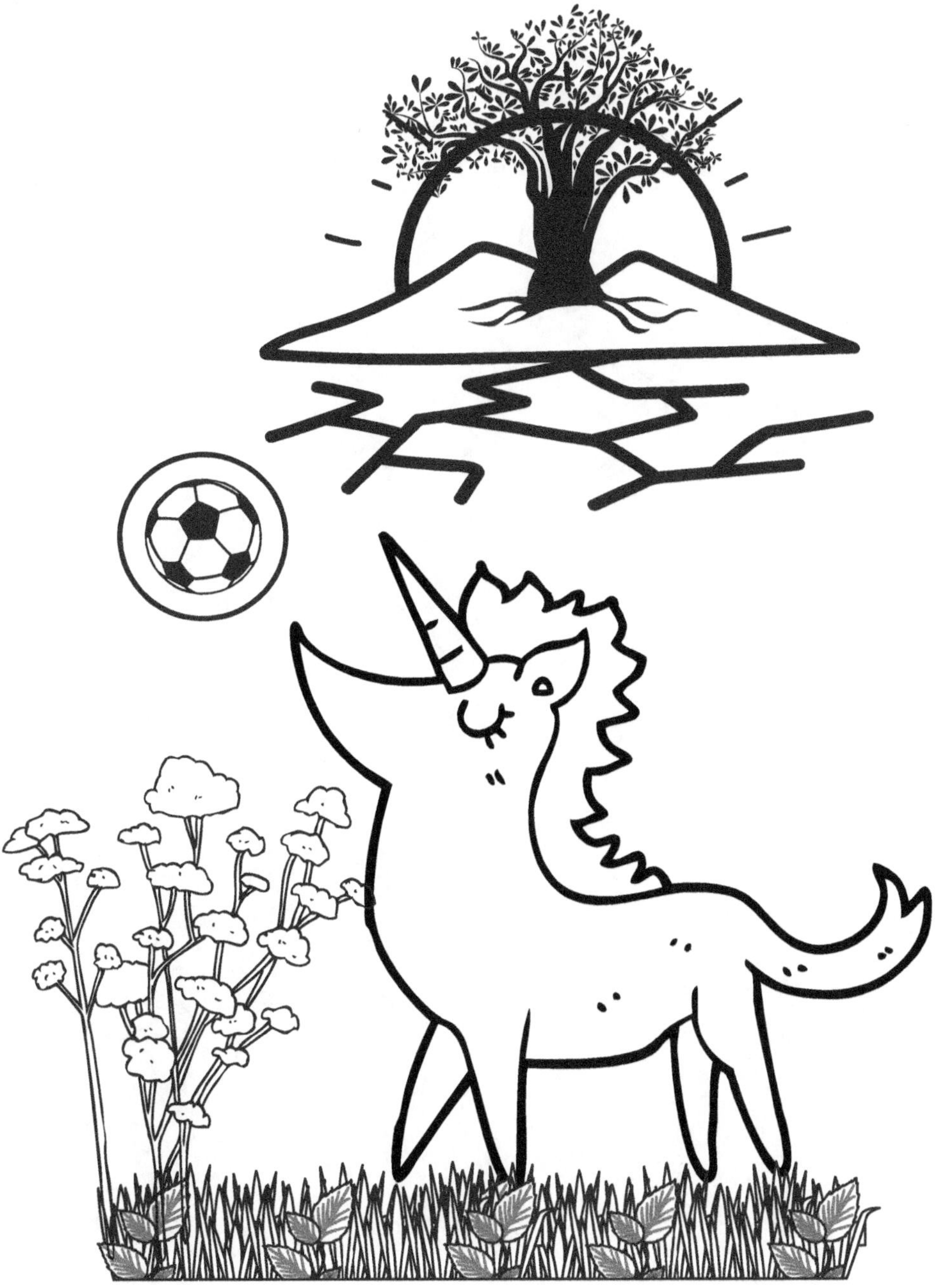

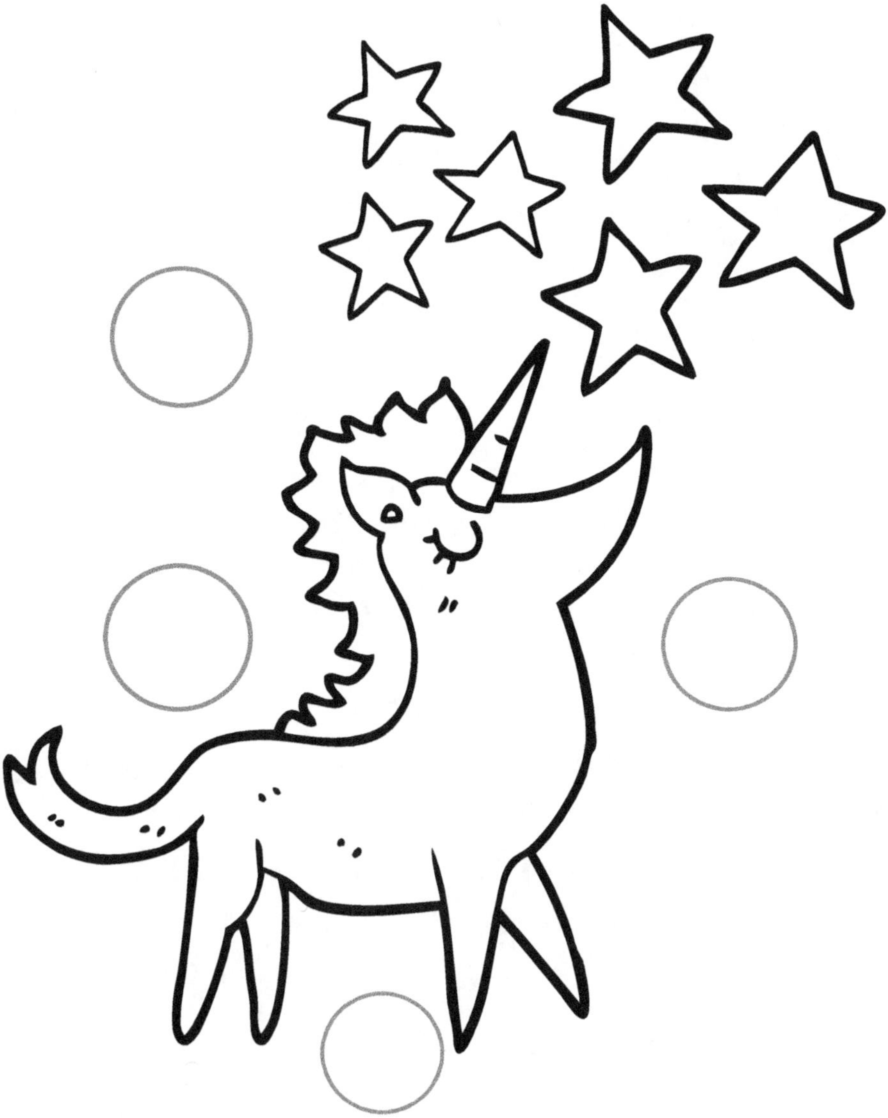

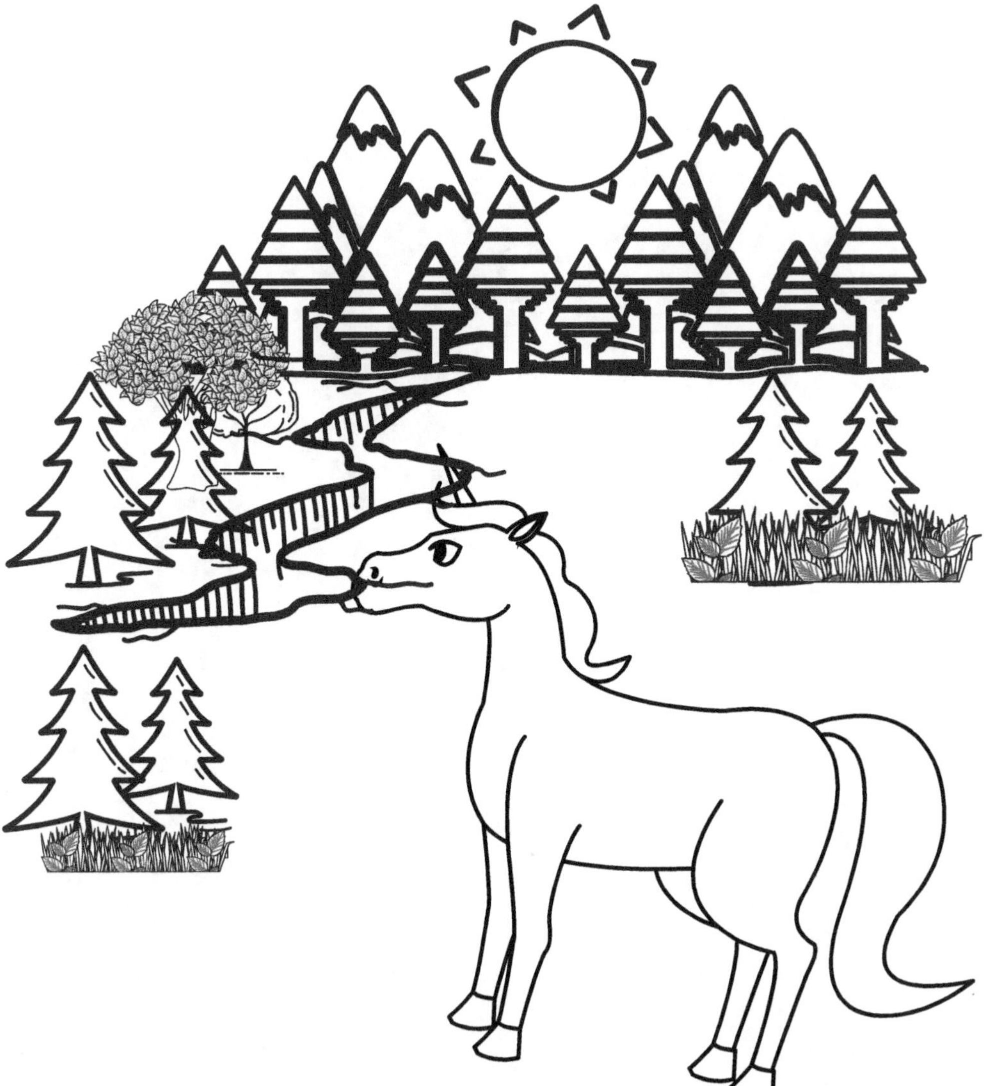

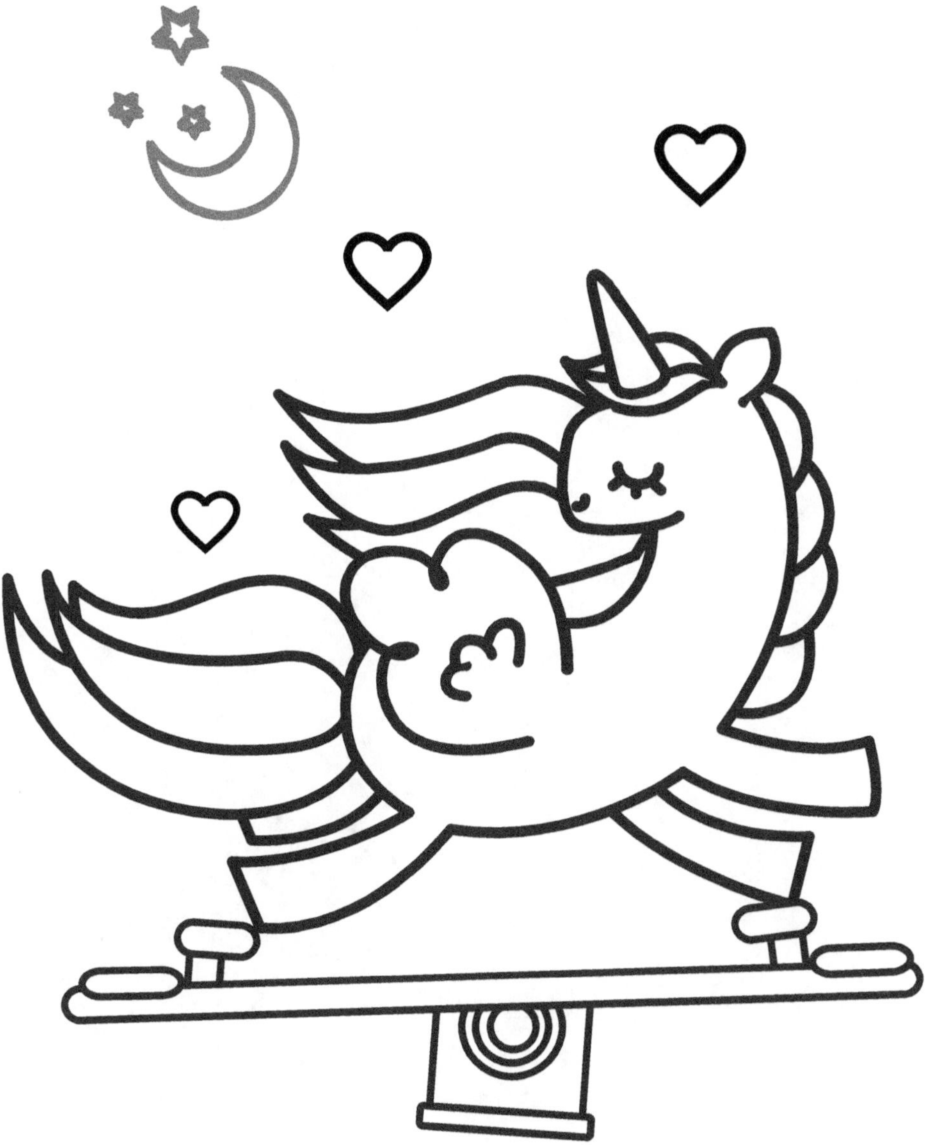

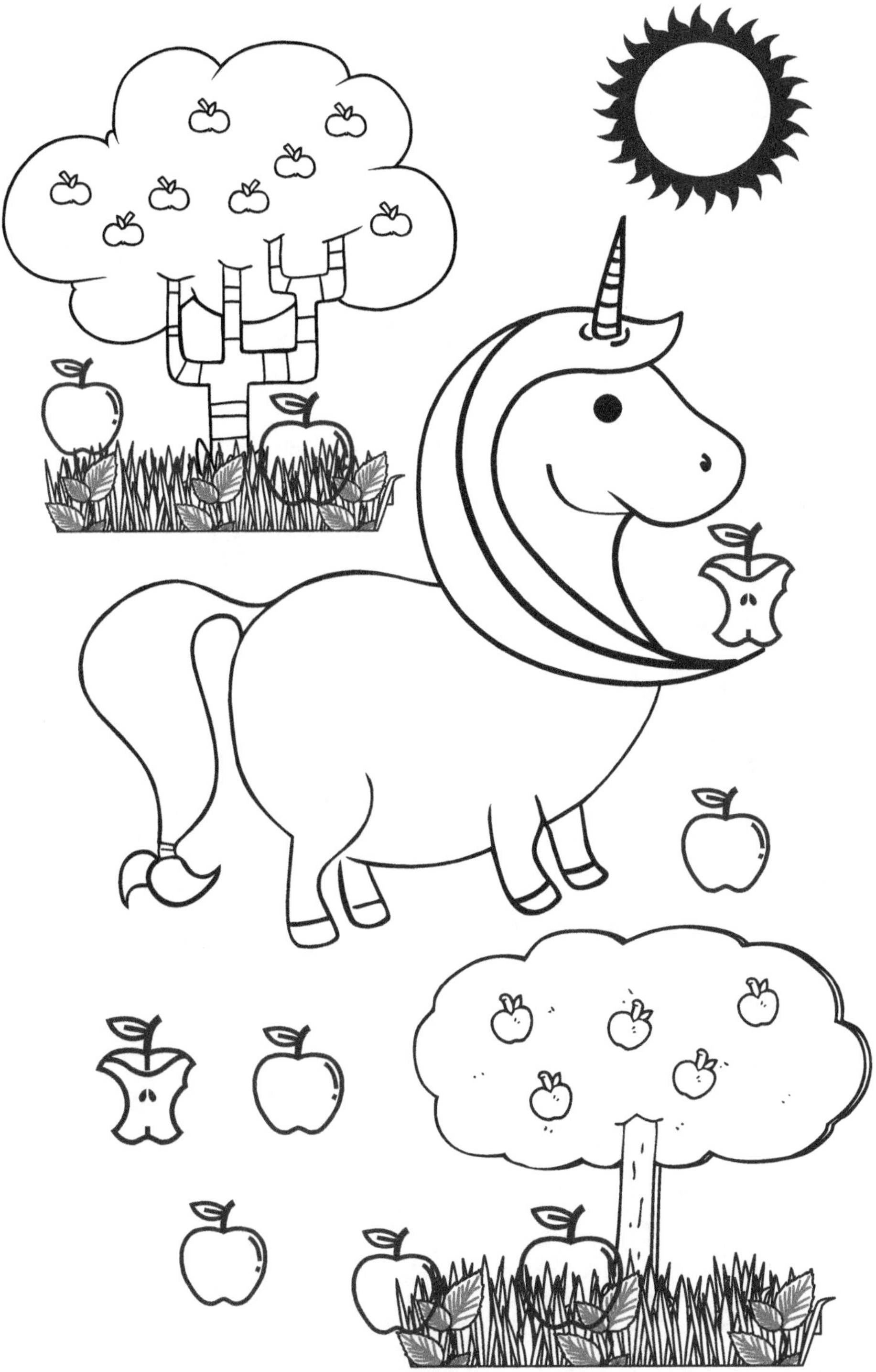

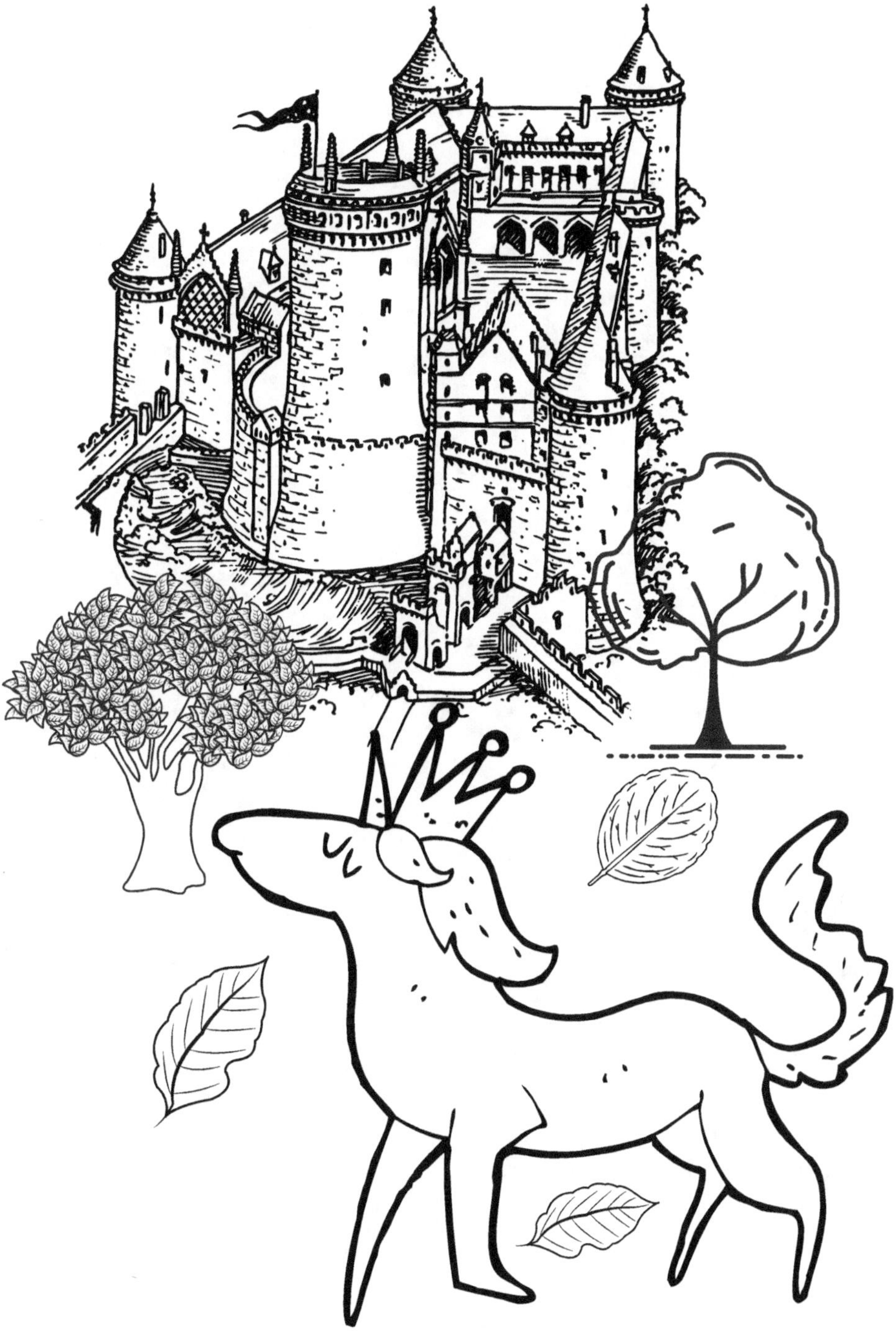

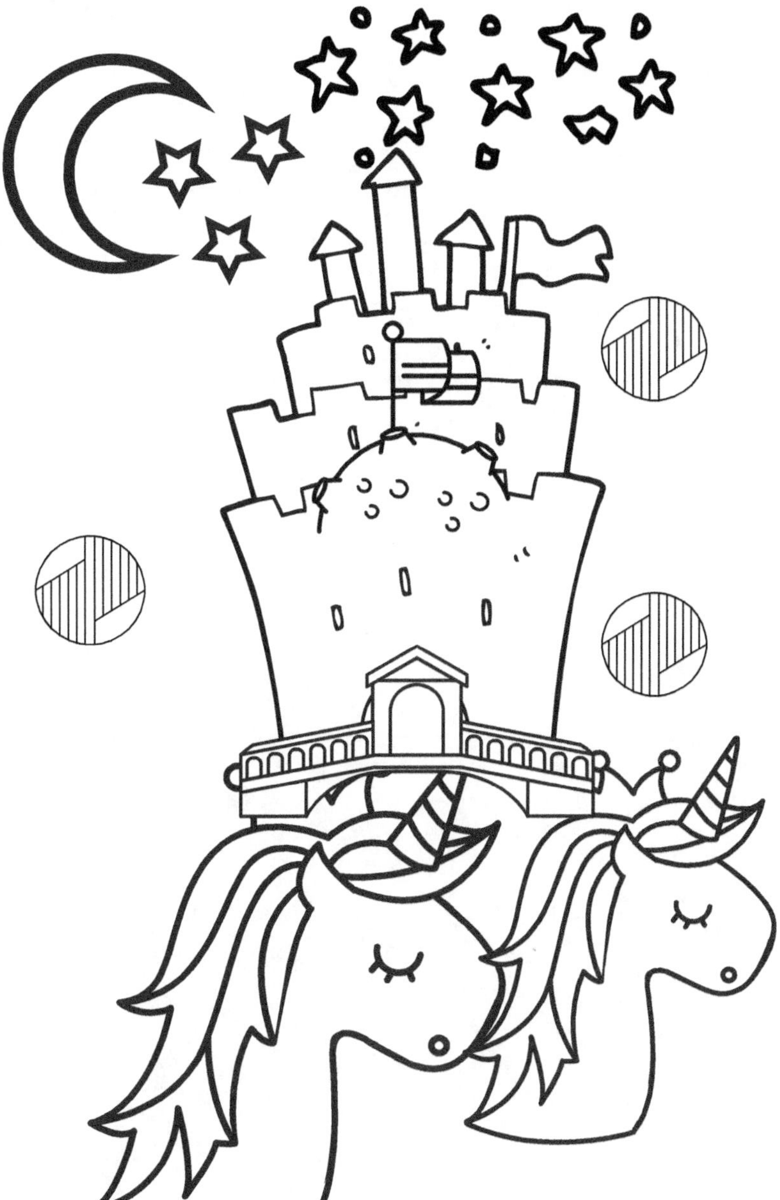

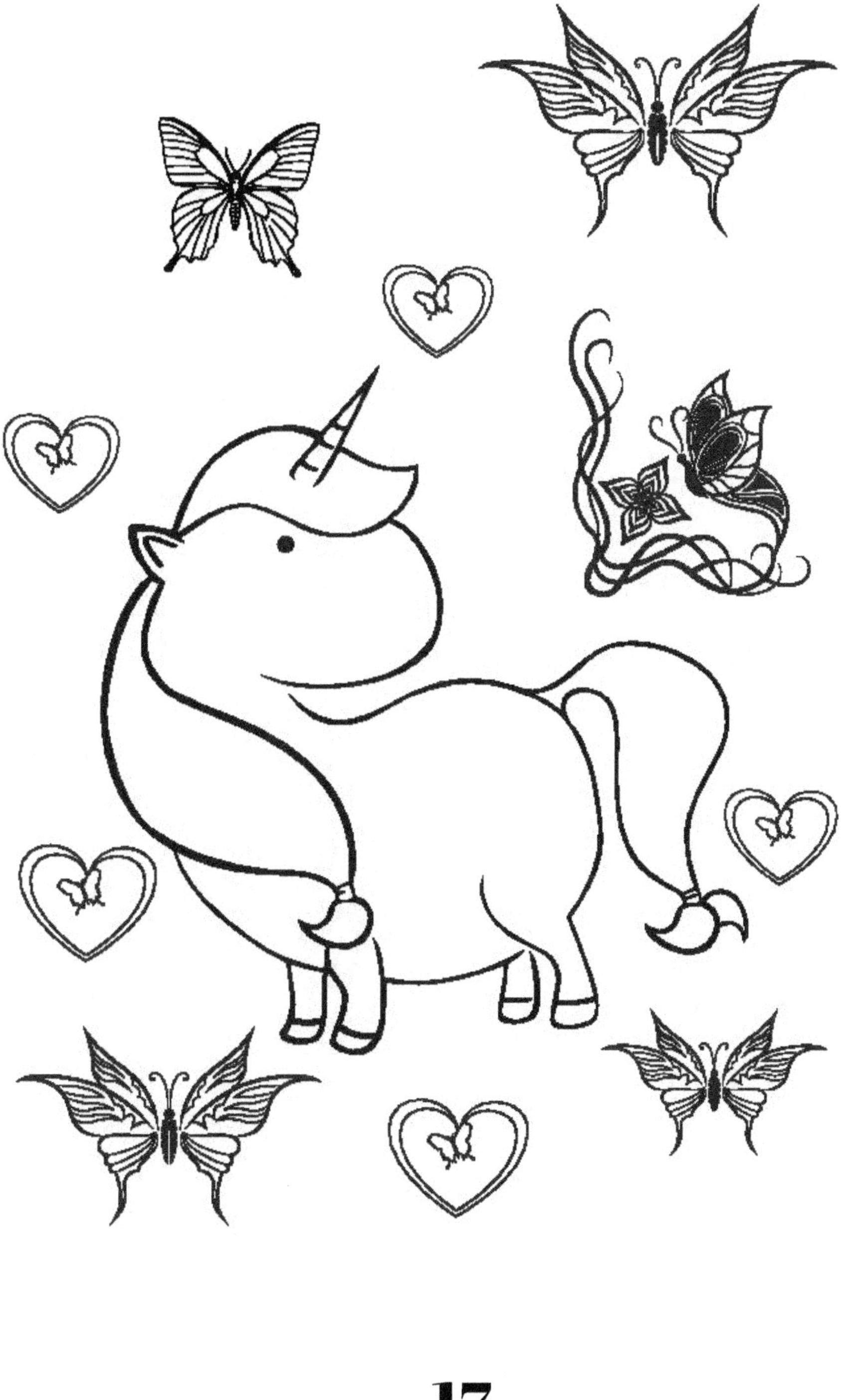

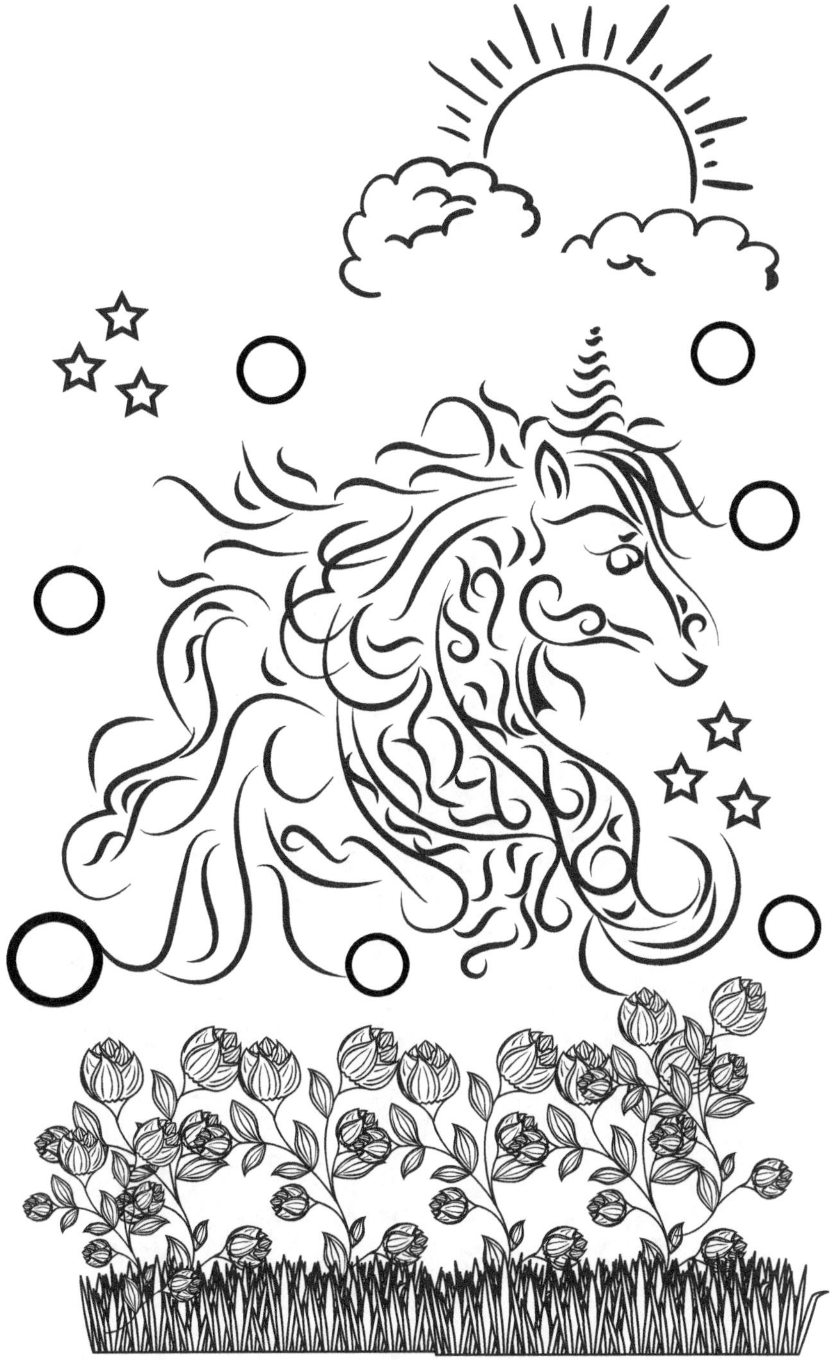

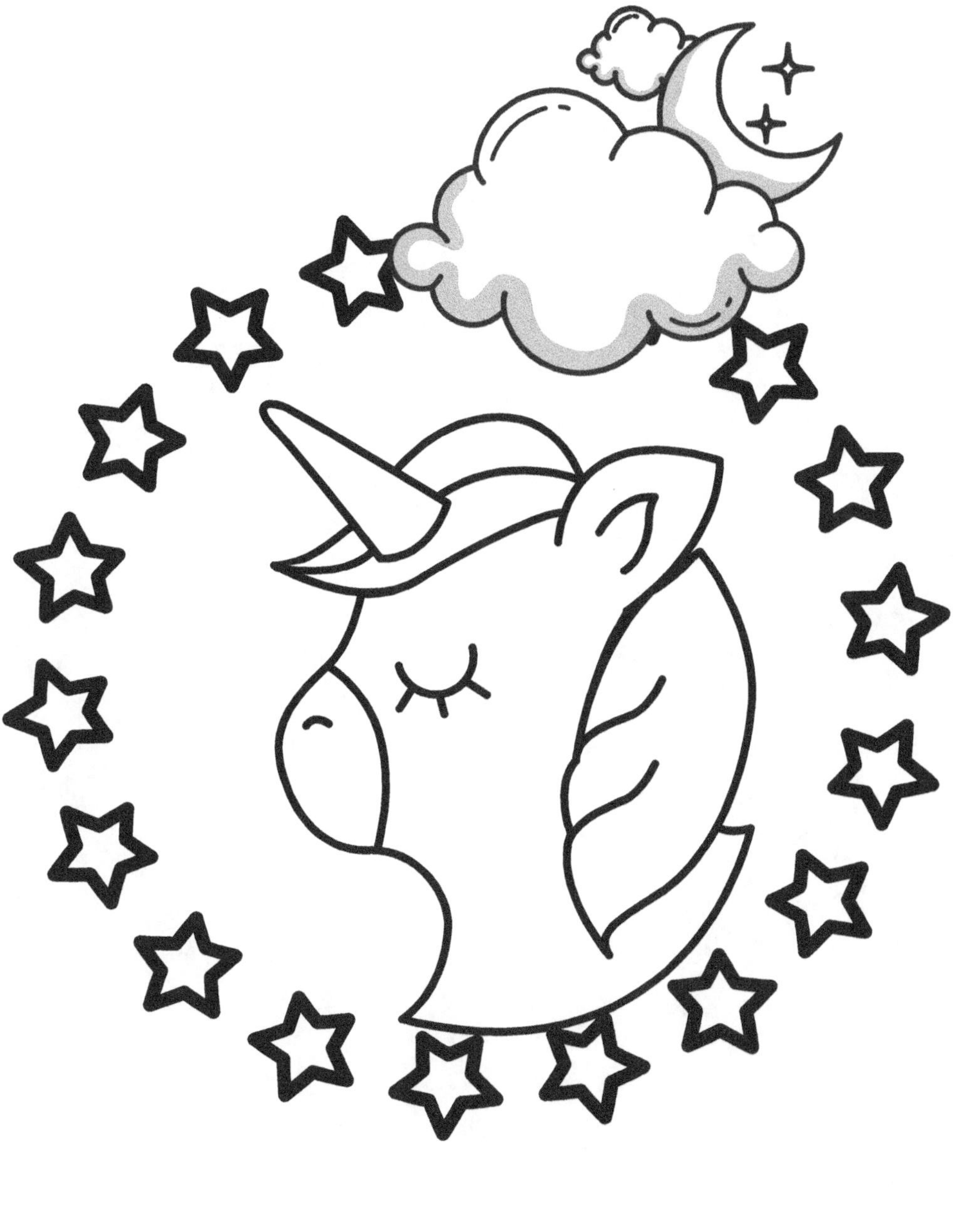

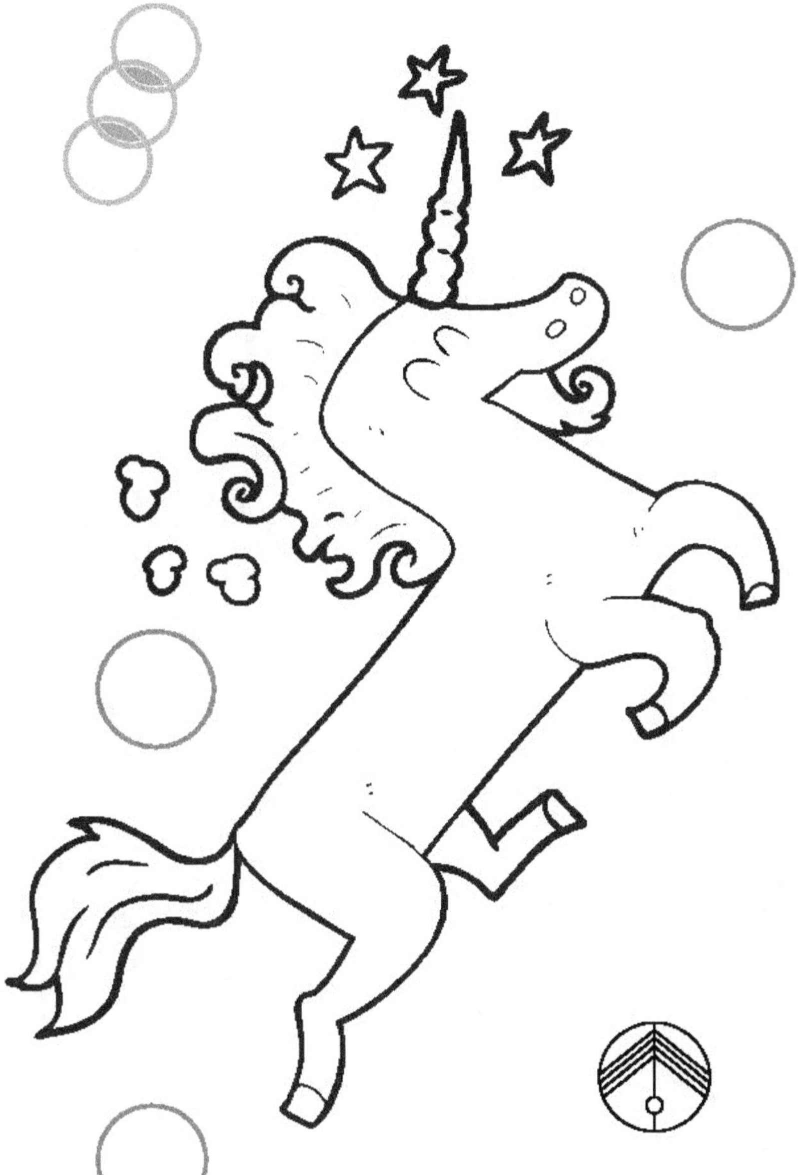

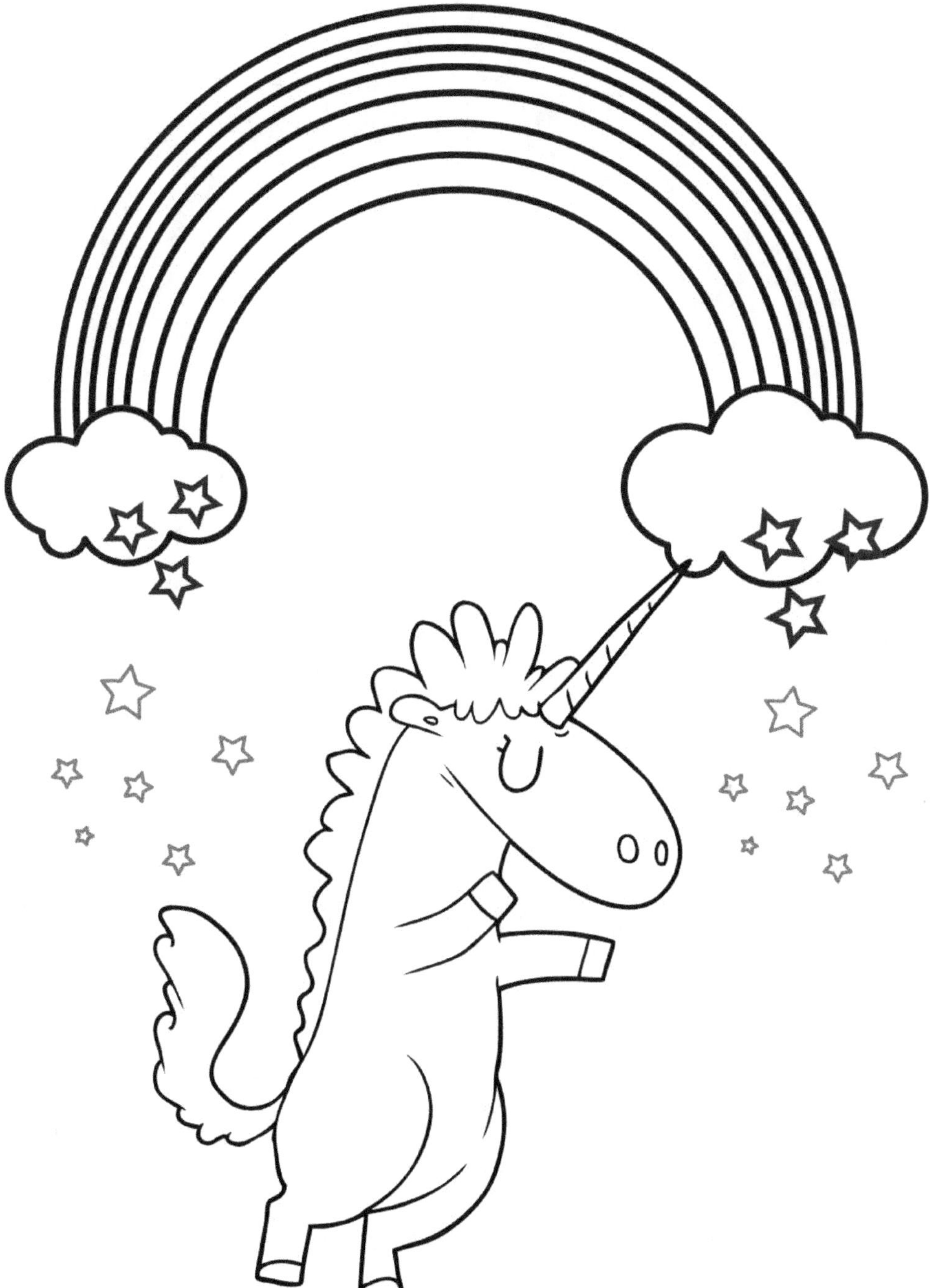

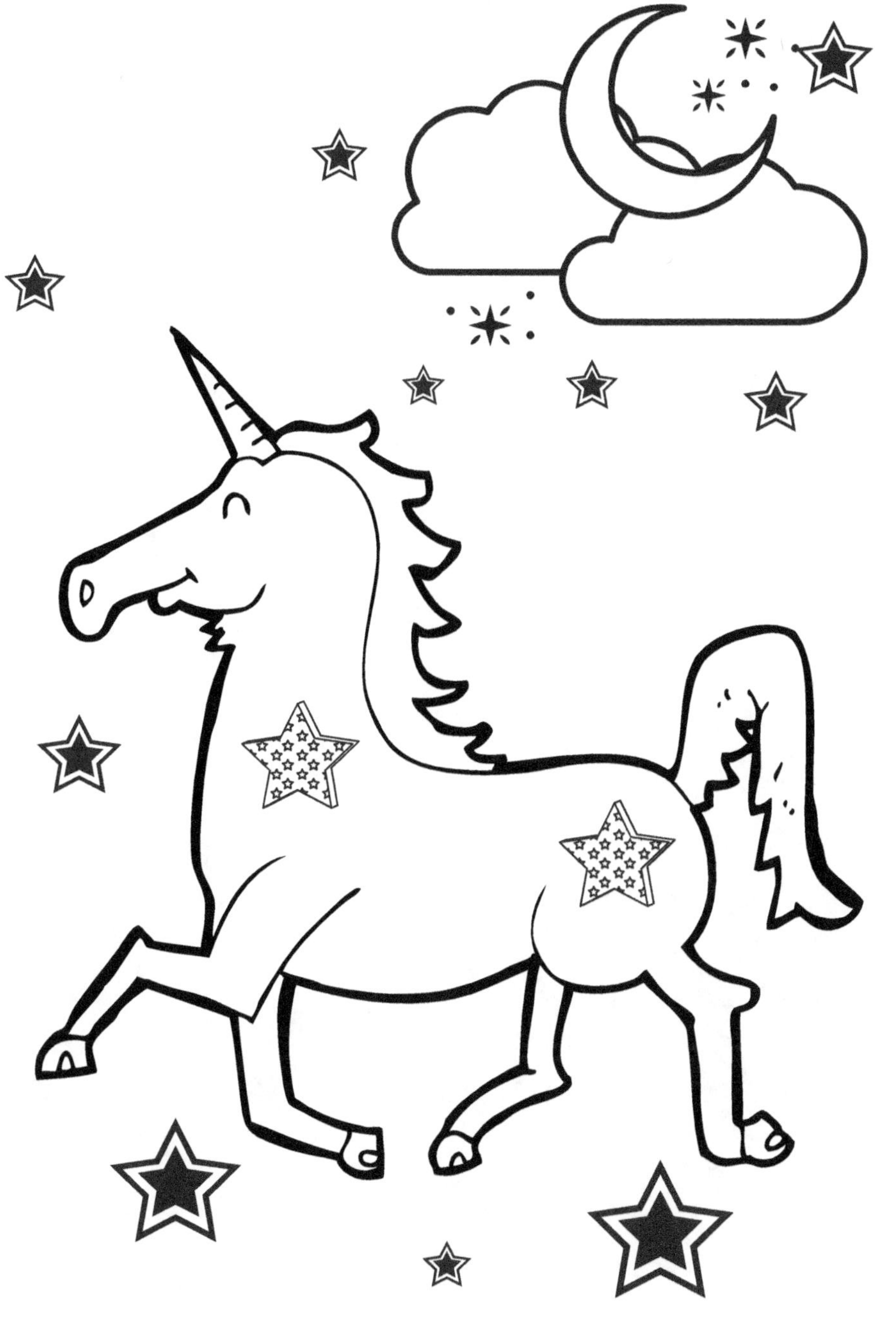

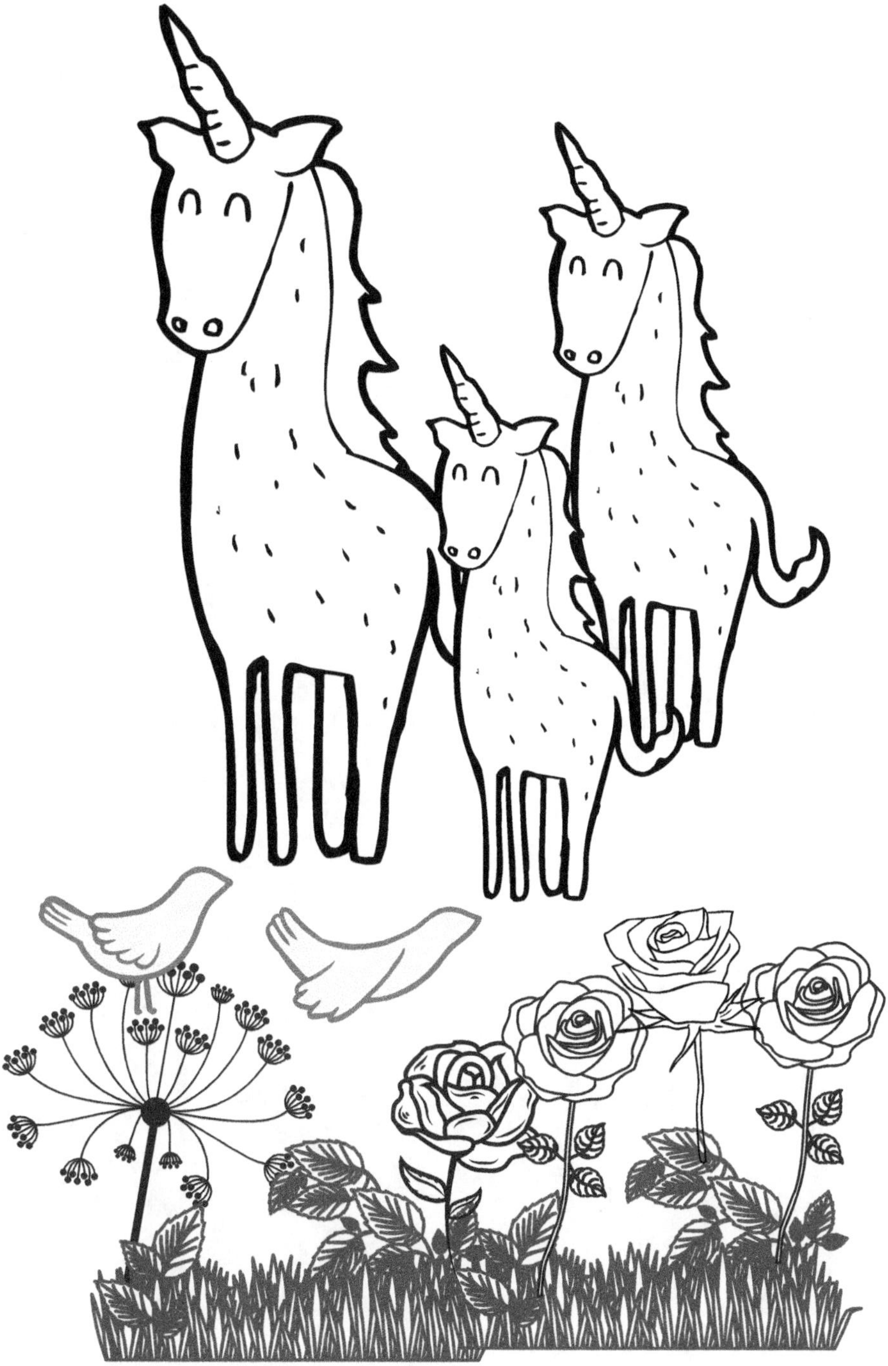

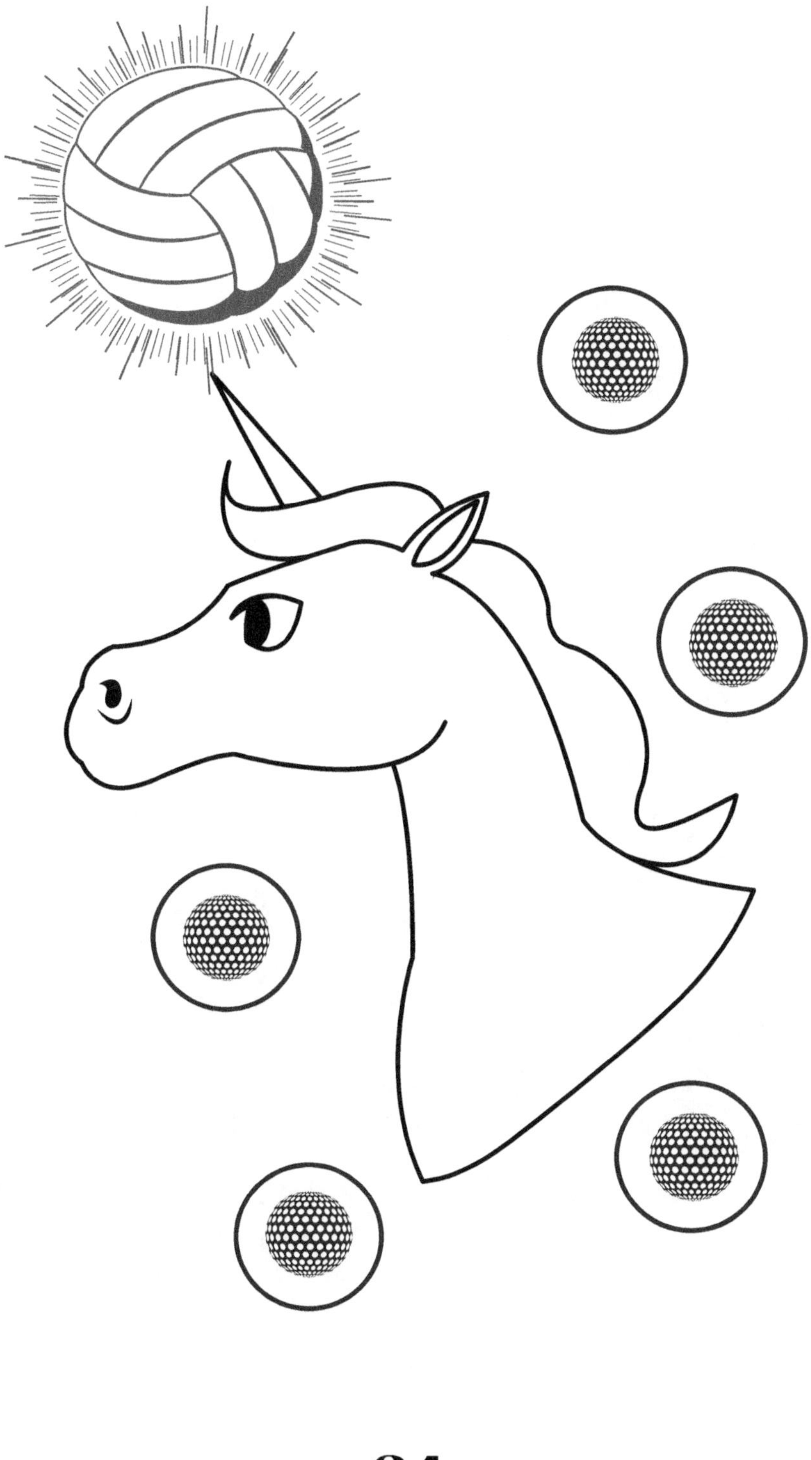

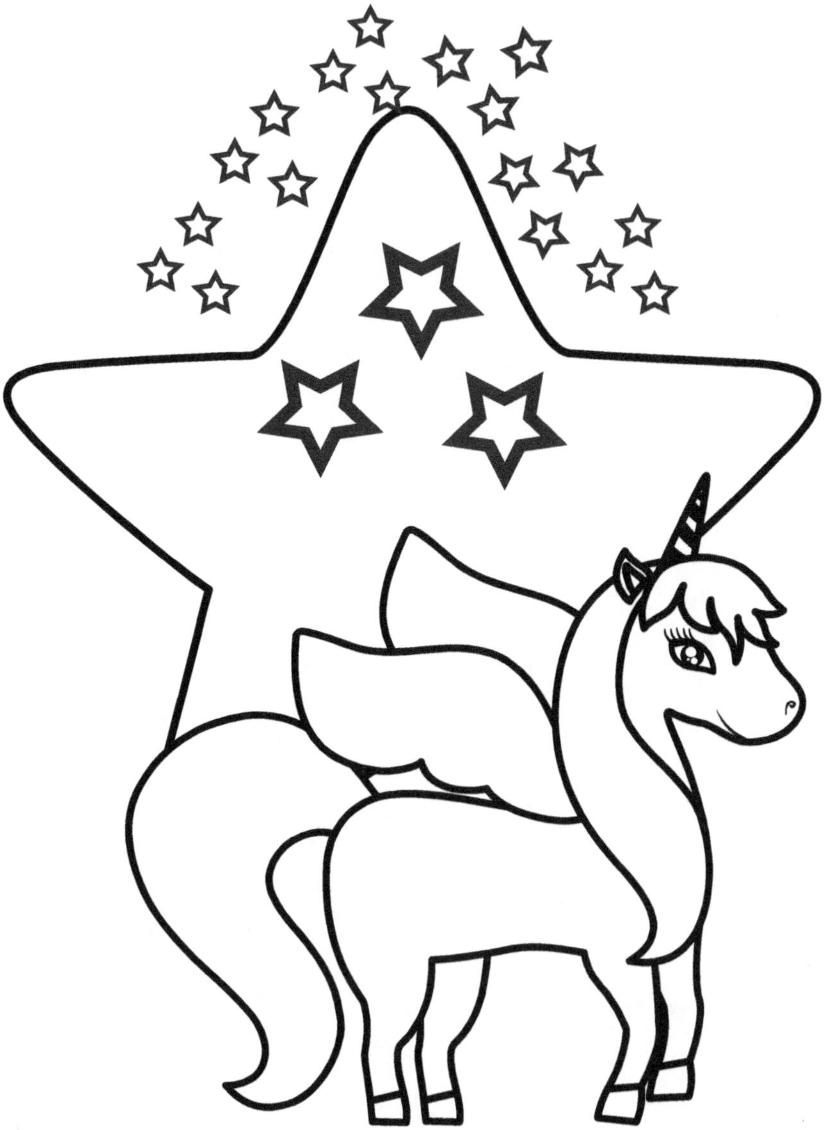

www.ingramcontent.com/pod-product-compliance
Lightning Source LLC
Chambersburg PA
CBHW050314220526
45465CB00005B/1992
* 9 7 9 8 6 1 2 3 4 2 9 3 9 *